MW01241130

Love From Me To You
You
A collection of poetry

Linnette R. Alston

DEDICATION

This is dedicated to all those who believe in true love. True love does exist for those who believe.

In loving memory of my dad Linwood Alston.

CONTENTS

Acknowledgments   i

1   Pillow Talk   Pg #1

2   Questioning My Heart   Pg #2

3   The Kiss of a Stranger   Pg #3

4   Since We Last Spoke   Pg #4

5   Will You Think of Me   Pg #5

6   Under Siege   Pg #6

7   What is Love   Pg #7

8   Just in Case   Pg #8

9   Do You Remember   Pg #9

10   Thinking of You and I   Pg #10

11	One Time Love	Pg #11
12	Reversal of Love	Pg #12
13	Remember	Pg #13
14	Let Me	Pg #14
15	Love's Moment	Pg #15
16	Easy for Me	Pg #16
17	Love's Magic	Pg #17
18	The Man in my Life	Pg #18
19	From My Heart to Yours	Pg #19

ACKNOWLEDGMENTS

First, I would like to thank God for all the blessings and the gifts He has given. I thank God for all the doors He has opened to make this book possible. I want to thank my mother Arnita Alston, my brothers Derrick Alston and Kevin Alston for all their love and support that they have given me though out the years. Thank you family for pushing me and inspiring me to make this book happen. I want to thank my extended family and friends. Special thanks to Sandra Lee, Shawnee Newell, Paula Price, and Stephine Richardson. You ladies have been my sounding board and your support has been invaluable. I can't forget my friend and mentor Debbie Forman who inspired me to have the courage to take the shot. Lastly, I want to thank the love of my life Deardeary Sutton who inspires me to love. Thank you Dee for your love and support. I love you!

Pillow Talk

Would it tell you of the pain I endured
The countless tears and no one to reassure
The wonder you would embark
If my pillow could talk

Would it tell you of happy times of days gone by
The continuous smile that could light up the sky
The wonder you would embark
If my pillow could talk

Would it tell you of my intense fears or love
The overwhelming feelings that keeps me looking above
The wonder you would embark
If my pillow could talk

Would it tell secret desires that I hold deep inside
Would it uncover failures that I try desperately to hide
The wonder you would embark
If you my pillow could talk

Would it tell of the love my heart so closely holds
If it had a voice would it speak loudly and bold
The wonder you would embark
If my pillow would dare to talk

Questioning My Heart

How did I get here a place of serenity
A place where loud moments find peace
And the most unbearable and horrific sights
Somehow in its mist there is a quiet beauty

When did I get here a time of utter bliss
Moments of pleasure which have me spellbound
Time that seems unpredictable and strange
Calms and stands still with your tender kiss

What did I do to deserve such complete happiness
Did I wish upon a midnight star shinning so bright
Or did an angel take my prayer to an almighty God
I can't think of another reason why I am so blessed

I didn't believe in happily ever after I didn't want to try
Yet here I am believing and wishing for things I can't see
Stopping to smell the roses and finding truth in fairy tales
Could it be I am falling in love and you're the reason why

For these already answered questions I will find what's true
To ease my hearts intellect and ease my already blown mind
I'll look in a place strange yet familiar and I'll take my time
Because everything I need and want can be found in you

The Kiss Of A Stranger

Like a predator about to devour its prey
Your inviting glance now has me at bay
I find myself in paralyzing danger
From the kiss of a stranger

Your powerful essence renders me helpless
The animalistic attraction that makes me breathless
I find myself in immediate danger
From the kiss of a stranger

Here I am your willing victim
Awaiting the presence of you to enter my system
I find myself in heart pounding danger
From the kiss of a stranger

Now submitting to your will
You systematically go in for the kill
I find myself in present danger
From the kiss of my handsome stranger

Since We Last Spoke

Since we last spoke I have been a little blue
Can't think of why it could be maybe just missing you
Since we last spoke my heart has not been the same
Could it be that things have changed and I am to blame

Since we last spoke my mind has drawn a complete blank
Not sure if it's crazy or memory loss that I should thank
Since we last spoke my vision is slightly blurred and unclear
Never imagined I'd miss hearing your voice or having you near

Since we last spoke can't hear the melody to a song
Guess I am not in that place that I feel I belong
Since we last spoke my sensations have no special tingle
With friends and loved ones I find it hard to mingle

With you I found a special place that I thought was mine
In the blink of an eye things changed at the drop of a dime
It is safe to say that my feelings my heart is completely broke
And all of this occurred....since we last spoke

Will You Think Of Me

As the sun begins to kiss the earth
And echoes of yesterday fade away
As new exciting thoughts give birth
Will you think of me today

The afternoon hot and steamy
Your soul feels it may catch on fire
Suddenly at the point of feeling dreamy
Will you think of me and feel the desire

Evening now mysterious and dark
In a moment passion ignites
Pleasure awaits now to embark
Will you think and dream of me tonight

Your thoughts now give way to slumber
And thoughts of me surprisingly have not gone
Now you discover you are not alone
As you think of me and remember.

Under Siege

Invade my heart with your love
Allow your spirit to shine through
Shower me like rain from above
Let our love glisten as morning dew

Stalk me with your loving presence
Let the hunter become the hunted
Take control with your dominating essence
As your prey make me feel wanted

Conquer me with masculine strength
Keep my gentle feminine wiles at bay
Torture me with sensual charm at any length
Until night gives in ultimately into day

You have captured me every part
I surrender all that I am to you
My mind body and yes my heart
Just love me in the special way you do

What Is Love

Love songs the words dance in my head
The melody each time I hear is brand new
Love is the thought of you

The smell of flowers during a summer day
The sky is beautiful and a perfect shade of blue
Love is the atmosphere of you

The quiet sound of the sea
The stillness that has your heart subdued
Love is the peacefulness of you

Care given with every thought
So many wonderful things you do
Love is the spirit of you

What is love
The answer rings true
Love is simply you

Just In Case

Just in case you didn't know
It breaks my heart to see you go
To know that our love is no more
The tears they come like rain
From my eyes they pour

Just in case you didn't see
Just how much you completed me
Like a riddle ready to be solved
Because of your love I evolved

Just in case you didn't know
Your love in my heart I'll always hold
The love you gave so freely
The love that allowed me to be me

Losing you has caused me pain
But I know one day I may love again
The essence of you won't be replaced
I'll hold you in my heart….just in case

Do You Remember

Do you remember strolls in the park
As the breeze kissed your face in the dark
When life was care free and easy
And the simplest sound gave a melody

Do you remember holding hands along the beach
The waves caressing your soul with its pulsating reach
A time when life gave flight
And love shinned as the hopeful light

Do you remember places unknown to us
Giving into fate allowing your heart to trust
When adventure was the guide
And feelings unknown would never hide

Memory is the echo of our minds
Linking the past to the present
The common thread that binds
Time with all its splendor
Can you recall...do you remember

Thinking Of You and I

As I think of you and I
My mind wonders of a tranquil waterfall
The beauty the peace the melodic sound
Which beacons my heart with its call

As I think of you and I
My mind compares it to the beauty of a flower
The purity the perfectness the simple aroma
Renders you helpless under its hypnotic power

As I think of you and I
My mind finds green meadows
The openness the quietness the unspoken calm
A divines that heaven only knows

Warmth tenderness an undying love
The beauty I see in my mind's eye
Can only be given from God above
Beautiful feelings as I think of you and I

One Time Love

You swept me off my feet
I was your damsel in distress
A look from your eyes made me complete
The warmth from you put all my fears to rest

You made me look within myself
To find the self I once knew
You encourage me like no one else
It was then I fell in love with you

Your dried my tears with a touch
A touch with warmth filled with care
I didn't think I would care so much
A moment in time we'll always share

You looked at me and wanted more
More communication love and time
I was afraid to unlock love's door
Amazing things changed at the drop of a dime

The moment in time we came to know
As quickly as it came it went
Sad the feelings had no chance to grow
With beautiful memories and time well spent

Looking back now it seems so clear
That you were a gift from the heavens above
I pray God will keep you safe and near
My dear friend and one time love

Reversal of Love

You said you wanted my quality time
You said you wanted it for keeps
You wanted to share so much with me
But shallow waters can't run deep

You said you wanted my caressing kisses
You said that you wanted my tingling touch
You wanted to stare in these eyes of love
Poetic yet empty words don't mean too much

You said you wanted to care for me
Your said you wanted to take care of my heart
You wanted to be in love with wonderful me
Your actions and words are more than worlds apart

The sweet nothings continue to ring in my ear
Hard to imagine you my blessing could be my curse
Loving you was so wonderful and seemingly easy
Never thought loving you would be in reverse

Remember

Remember that I love you
Don't allow your heart to forget
A love special that's not so new
A love of sacrifice and no regret

Remember that I adore you
More and more as days go by
It's funny how the attraction grew
Even though my heart tried hard to deny

Remember that I admire you
For your tenacity and sense of style
Through the silly things you do
You seem to make even heaven smile

Remember that I respect you
For the wonderful person you are
A friend that has proven to be true
My friend you will always be my heart

As time moves on one thing will remain
From January even through December
The love I feel now will still be the same
The love we share I will always remember

Let me

Let me be the first thought that enters your mind
The thought the envelopes your brain
A thought that causes your soul to unwind

Let me be that moment of time that makes you smile
The thought that makes you dance
Dancing endlessly for what seems to be an endless mile

Let me be the provider of warmth for an ugly and cold day
Allow me to melt all of your agonizing problems
Until every disappointment and pain has gone away

Let me be your gentle anchor upon the raging sea
To help keep you somewhat grounded
Bur never at any moment afraid to set you free

Let me show you an abundance of love intense and sweet
Let my love shower and yes penetrate you
From the top of your head down to your feet

Allow me to give all I have and let me do it freely
Grant me the time to show all you are to me
I can make you happy if you…let me

Love's Moment

From the moment I saw you
Love never entered my mind
Never thought I could say the word
Now love has me blind

From the moment we held hands
Trust suddenly became my guide
Giving in to multiple emotions
From my feeling now I can't hide

From the moment we shared our first kiss
My heart at the moment swelled
With such an intense feeling of love
It was in that moment I fell

From the moment we fell in love
You my friend became my lover
My heart and love I pledge to you
Never will I give my love to another

At this special moment in time
In this day that is magical and new
From this moment and the rest of my life
I'll always be in love with you

Easy For Me

It would be easy for me to say
That life has not been easy
I have had my share of heartaches
That is until the day you freed me

It would be easy for me to say
I don't want to trust another man
I can't make that uncertain journey
And here you are extending your hand

It would be easy for me to say
It's hard to let go of the past
The feeling of hurt and some guilt
But here you are and I let go at last

It would be easy for me to say
I'm scared to take the first step
The fear of falling has me bound
You offer love and devotion as my help

Give into your feelings I'll take care of you
And make beautiful each and every day
Being with you my fantasy comes true
Finally I am yours and it was easy to say

Love's Magic

Friends I am told make the best lovers
I never once thought the cliché was true
Never did I believe in four leaf clovers
Until the day I fell in love with you

The magic found in a shiny crystal ball
I always thought was a child's fairy tale
Love the secret potion that heals all
Has my unbelieving heart ready to set sail

Wishing and always hoping on a mystical star
Were for people I thought to be crazy
Now love's insanity has taken me so far
My clear intellectual sight has been made hazy

Love now has me miraculously spellbound
What an awesome and incurable mystery
The blissful happiness I have now found
With the enchanting love shared by you and me

So take me love on your powerful journey
To places where meadows are green and skies blue
To a place where all is filled with love's beauty
That magical place consumed with love me and you

The Man in my Life

You were there when I took my first step
You were there when I spoke my first word
You have always been there when I need help
You taught me to let my voice be heard

You were there to encourage me
When other said so often you can't
Allowing me to be what I wanted to be
You gave water to me a withering plant

Your love you continue to give freely
Without a thought or care
Your love surrounds me daily
Your love is precious and rare

As I reflect over the years
The good times and the bad
You have been there to dry my tears
And I am proud to call you Dad
So until Prince Charming makes me his wife
You Dad are the man in my life

From My Heart to Yours

From my heart to yours
When troubles never cease
Just look to the heavens
God will bring you peace

From my heart to yours
May love reign forever more
He died on the cross
And it's Jesus we should adore

From my heart to yours
I pray for you peace of mind
Whatever it maybe
Everything in God you'll find

Remember God loves you
When happiness make you heart soar
Let's all love one another
This is from my heart to yours

ABOUT THE AUTHOR

Linnette Alston, is the CEO of All for you Travel, works in the health care industry as a medical claims biller and is now an author. Linnette was born in Washington D.C and was raised in Littleton, North Carolina. For more information please go to my website lovefrommetoyou.com

Made in the USA
Middletown, DE
15 July 2023

35071129R00018